Truck Driver

Earning $50,000–$100,000 with a High School Diploma or Less

Announcer

Car Mechanic

Chef

Cosmetologist

DJ

Dog Groomer

Energizing Energy Markets:
Clean Coal, Shale, Oil, Wind, and Solar

Farming, Ranching, and Agriculture

Masseur & Massage Therapist

Personal Assistant

Presenting Yourself: Business Manners,
Personality, and Etiquette

Referee

The Arts: Dance, Music, Theater, and Fine Art

Truck Driver

Earning $50,000–$100,000
with a High School Diploma or Less

Truck Driver

CONNOR SYREWICZ

MASON CREST

Mason Crest
450 Parkway Drive, Suite D
Broomall, PA 19008
www.masoncrest.com

Printed in the United States of America.

First printing
9 8 7 6 5 4 3 2 1

Series ISBN: 978-1-4222-2886-9
ISBN: 978-1-4222-2900-2
ebook ISBN: 978-1-4222-8936-5

The Library of Congress has cataloged the
        hardcopy format(s) as follows:

            Library of Congress Cataloging-in-Publication Data

Syrewicz, Connor.
  Truck driver / Connor Syrewicz.
      pages cm. – (Earning $50,000 - $100,000 with a high school diploma or less)
  Includes bibliographical references and index.
  Audience: Grade 7 to 8.
      ISBN 978-1-4222-2900-2 (hardcover) – ISBN 978-1-4222-2886-9 (series) –
ISBN 978-1-4222-8936-5 (ebook)
 1. Truck drivers–Juvenile literature. 2. Trucking–Vocational guidance–Juvenile literature.
I. Title.
  HD8039.M795S97 2014
  388.3'24023–dc23
                                    2013011187

Produced by Vestal Creative Services.
www.vestalcreative.com

Contents

CHAPTER 1

Careers Without College

When Joanna Dunham sums up her fifteen years as a truck driver, she says "Good money, great experiences, and a lot of lessons learned."

She continues, "Truck drivers experience America in a way that most people could only dream of. We drive big, beautiful trucks, and we make good money doing it. It's a good way to make a living and if it suits your personality, you're on your way to making many of the best memories of your entire life. But," she adds, "it's not for everyone.

"You do not question whether or not this kind of job is right for you. You question whether or not you are the right kind of person for this job. The

Driving a truck requires patience and determination, as well as good driving skills.

TRUCK DRIVER

truth is that driving trucks isn't really just a job; it's how you live."

According to Joanna, the best truck drivers are **patient**, **independent**, **determined**, and hard working. They love adventure and like thinking quickly. "But most of all," Joanna says, "A good truck driver needs discipline. Traffic, weather, eating, sleeping, showering, fueling, getting work done on the truck; it takes a truck driver a long time to learn how to juggle everything.

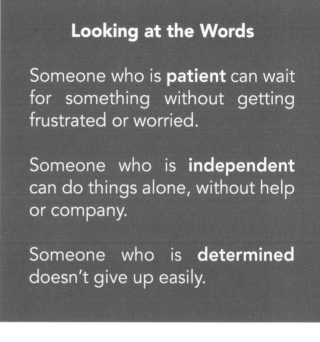

Looking at the Words

Someone who is **patient** can wait for something without getting frustrated or worried.

Someone who is **independent** can do things alone, without help or company.

Someone who is **determined** doesn't give up easily.

"You have to be willing to work long hours, sometimes with little sleep, and be willing to be away from home for weeks. You miss birthdays, holidays, and graduations. You have to be willing to deal with unexpected problems. But these are small compromises when you consider that you're providing an important service to people you can be proud of."

Trucks, Trucks, Trucks

Next time you buy something from the store take a moment to realize that there is at least a 70 percent chance that what you just bought was delivered by truck. Think of everything we want and need in our everyday lives. These things are called "goods" and goods come from all over

Truck drivers get used to driving through countless towns. The road ahead is the constant in their lives.

the world. The vehicles and people that have the responsibility of moving these goods are known as the "shipping **industry**." The shipping industry moves goods many ways—by plane, train, and boat—but trucks move more goods than any of these other ways combined.

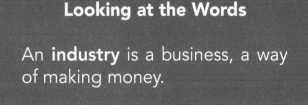

Looking at the Words

An **industry** is a business, a way of making money.

If you happen to be riding along on one of America's highways and you pass a big truck, turn your head and look at the driver: you'll be looking at one of the 3.5 million truck drivers who live and drive on America's 4 million miles of road each and every day. You will be looking at one of the many people responsible for keeping most of America's goods moving.

These men and women who have had a hand in getting you many of the things you need and love have many strengths in common. But one thing most of them don't have is a college education.

The College Question

Joanna didn't always know that a college education would not be the best choice for her, but while going to high school, her choice became clear. "I always enjoyed learning," she says, "and it was while I was in high school that I discovered *what* I wanted to learn. It just wasn't something you could be taught in a classroom."

For most young people, high school is an influential time and place. Young people are given more responsibilities and challenged by new ideas, experiences, and expectations. Most students, by this time, are

Graduating from college is a great achievement that can lead to success in life—but it's not right for everyone.

finally old enough to begin to use their free time and curiosity to explore new hobbies and interests. Both in and out of high school, young people are given the opportunity to learn about themselves and the world. But even though no two young people learn and grow alike, as students prepare to graduate high school, they are all asked the same question: "Is college the best choice for you?"

The answer to this question, for many high school graduates today, is "yes." In 2011, nearly seven out of every ten students who graduated high school went on to attend college. But even though this may be the *popular* choice, it may not always be the *best* choice.

According to CNN, the average student, in 2012, graduated college nearly $27,000 in debt, and half of all college graduates could either not find a job or ended up finding a job for which they didn't even need a college degree. According to the United States Bureau of Labor Statistics, many high-paying jobs do not require a college education, although most of them do still require additional training.

A good alternative to a college degree might be to attend a training program or "vocational" school—a school that trains you for a specific career but is shorter and much cheaper than a traditional four-year college. "I went to a driving school to learn how to drive a truck," Joanna says. "It was very cheap, a few thousand dollars, and I was able to pay for it without any loans. A lot of trucking companies will train you for free or give you back the money that you spent on going to trucking school. I didn't see why I would want to go to school for four years and, after that time, owe someone else a lot of money."

So, should you go to college? That's an important question, one that every high school student should ask. There are a lot of options out there, and one of the best decisions that a student can make is to get educated about education. Ask yourself: "What do I love to do? What are my hobbies? What do I have a passion for? Do I need to go to college to

If you enjoy tinkering with engines and being around vehicles of various sorts, you might enjoy a career as a truck driver.

get the skills that I need to be successful? How can I eventually earn a living doing what I love?"

Learning Outside the Classroom

"It wasn't because high school was hard," Joanna says when she explains why she decided not to get a college education. She got good grades, enjoyed making friends, liked her teachers, and understood the importance of what she was learning in school—but it was during her after-school hours that Joanna discovered what she would eventually want to devote herself to: driving trucks.

Of course, Joanna did not start out in the driver's seat of a truck. Though it was not the kind of skill that she could learn at her high school, Joanna discovered that driving trucks requires training, skill, and a lot of **dedication**.

Joanna started fixing cars and trucks before she even had her license to drive them. Her father was a mechanic, and growing up, she was able to see the satisfaction and sense of **achievement** her father got from fixing cars. "It was my father's enthusiasm in cars and trucks that got me interested in them," Joanna says, but it wasn't until she was in high school that her father first

Looking at the Words

Dedication means you stick with something. You give it your best shot.

When you feel a sense of **achievement**, you feel you have done something good, something important. Achievement makes you feel good about yourself.

Careers Without College

Some community colleges offer truck-driving programs. These trucks are used for driver training at Northeast Community College in Norfolk, Nebraska.

helped her begin to explore this interest. "My father and I took apart an old car that was left on our property by the former owner of our house. It was so worn-out, there was no way we could fix it, but my father let me use his tools, and I loved taking it apart, looking at how the parts were put together and imagining the engine run. After school, I started riding my bike over to my father's garage. I'd ask him questions and ask if I could help. I learned a lot from him."

Once Joanna received her driver's license, her hobby soon became a **passion**. "I thought I might want to become a mechanic but that was before I was behind the wheel," Joanna says. "I am still pretty good with

a wrench," she adds, "but driving is what I love."

Driving laws are different in each state, but growing up in New York, Joanna was able to get her permanent driver's license when she was seventeen. "I was in high school then and even though a lot of my friends had licenses, I was one of the only people who had a car.

"There wasn't much to do where I was growing up, so when we were bored, we would go for a drive. Driving became the way I relaxed, the way I took time to think, and the way I learned how to deal with stress. It wasn't long before I was thinking of some way to turn this hobby into a career."

Joanna, like many people who are good at their jobs, decided to turn her passion into a career.

The History of Trucking

Alexander Winton, a Scottish immigrant living and working in Cleveland, invented the semi-truck in 1899. He began his career making bicycles and then moved to working on some of the first automobiles, what were called at the time "horseless carriages." He built the first semi because he needed a way to transport these early vehicles.

CHAPTER 2

What Do Truck Drivers Do?

Truck drivers travel the whole country without paying a cent; they drive one of the most powerful machines on the road; they look through their windshield and see a constantly changing movie in front of them; they go to beautiful corners of the country that most of us have never even heard of; they get to be somewhere new every single day. They move, travel, voyage, wander, journey. In short: they drive.

Although driving is a big part of the job, being a

There are many different kinds of trucks, each with its own kind of driver and its own set of responsibilities.

professional truck driver doesn't mean that driving is all they do. Not only is there more to the job than driving, there are many different kinds of drivers, each with their own particular roles and responsibilities.

Long-Haul Truck Drivers

Mike and Rhonda Pulaski would probably agree with Joanna when she says that "driving trucks isn't just a job; it's how you live." Mike and Rhonda are known as "long-haul" drivers in the trucking industry. Long-haul drivers are the people we usually think of when we think of truck drivers. They do long-distance driving and spend a lot of time away from home. Technically, long-haul drivers can drive any kind of truck, but in most cases, they drive large trucks with eighteen wheels, also known as "semis."

Most long-haul drivers spend about four or five weeks driving and only a few days at home in between. Almost all truck drivers begin their careers as long-haul drivers. Married couples, like Mike and Rhonda, are not uncommon to the trucking industry, but most long-haul truckers drive alone. "All of the new guys start as long-haul drivers because you have to be able to drive a semi," Mike says, "and driving a semi isn't like driving any other kind of vehicle."

According to Mike, driving a semi is especially difficult because your truck is attached to a fifty-three-foot trailer and can weigh over forty tons when loaded with cargo. "Besides the size," Rhonda adds, "the brakes on a semi are much harder to use. There are more gears in the engine and

Long-haul drivers spend day after day driving, carrying loads across the country. It can be exhausting work.

about a thousand other small differences. You have to know what to do when going up or down a hill, how to turn in narrow streets, how to maneuver in traffic, and how to back up safely."

"But being a truck driver isn't only learning how to drive the truck," Mike puts in. "We also have to take care of the truck, ourselves and others on the road. For example, every time we want to take the truck out on the road, we have to do a pre-trip inspection." A pre-trip inspection involves checking the entire truck from front bumper to back bumper, making sure nothing is wrong with the engine, brakes, or trailer. "Many truck drivers complain about the number of tasks, other than driving, that we are responsible for," Mike says, "but Rhonda and I take pride in our pre-trip inspections. Our semi is practically our home, and we enjoy making sure that our home is in good shape."

Mike and Rhonda drive together not only because they enjoy the lifestyle but also because driving as a team allows them to drive for more hours a day than someone who is driving alone. "When we are out on the road, we have to keep track of the time we spend doing anything," Mike explains, "stopping, sleeping, eating, putting fuel in the truck. To keep a driver from getting too tired while they drive, there are laws that stop a single driver from driving more than eleven hours a day. Keeping track of our day lets us show that we are driving legally, and having Rhonda here means that we can legally do about double the driving a day if we wanted to that a single driver could do."

Owner-Operators

Other than the convenience of being able to work longer hours, Mike and Rhonda drive together because they hope to one day own their own truck. "We're making payments to the company we're working for

Owning an enormous vehicle like this one can be a huge responsibility—but it can also allow the driver/owner to make a lot more money.

in order to own the semi that we are driving now," Rhonda says. "Many companies have programs like this, where part of the money that you are paid goes toward buying your truck. It is a great way to become independent and start making more money."

If Mike and Rhonda own their own truck, they will be known as "owner-operators,"

Looking at the Words

When something is **leased**, that means you have a contract that allows you to use that thing in return for paying money every month or year. Leasing means almost the same thing as renting.

which simply means that the owner of the truck also operates it. There are many reasons to become an owner-operator. Owner-operators are in control of what kind of cargo they carry, where they would like to work, how many hours a day they work, and how long they want to be at home. Owner-operators fall into two categories: independent and **leased**.

Independent owner-operators are truck drivers who have turned their career into a business. They sometimes own more trucks than the one that they drive, which is called a "fleet" of trucks, and they generally make the most money of any drivers in the trucking industry, oftentimes more than $100,000 a year. But despite the great money and freedom that comes with being an independent owner-operator, owning your own truck and driving independently can be a very difficult life. Not only do the drivers have to pay for all the costs of driving a large truck on a daily basis, but if anything goes wrong—an accident on the road or a ticket from a police officer—they won't have the support of a large company to help them.

This is why some owner-operators decide to lease themselves and their trucks. Leasing gives an owner-operator many of the benefits of

Tanker truck drivers carry all sorts of liquids. This driver brought fresh drinking water to flood victims.

working for a trucking company. Although owner-operators who lease generally make less money than independent drivers, leasing still gives truck drivers the same freedom as owning their own trucks without all of the worries and added responsibilities that come from owning your own business.

"It can be tough," Mike says, "to choose what kind of driving is right for you. But if you have the personality for it, truck driving offers a lot of opportunities for making great money with more freedom than someone can have with a traditional job."

Other Kinds of Truck Drivers

Although most of the truck drivers on the road are long-haul drivers, there are many other kinds of truck drivers out there. Regional and local drivers, for example, do not drive nearly as far as a long-haul driver, and they get to go home most nights. They too work long hours, though, and they generally make much less money than long-haul drivers.

Another kind of driver drives trucks that are specially made to hold special cargo. For example, pulling a tanker involves driving a truck very much like a semi, but instead of a trailer, a tanker pulls a large container made to hold different kinds of liquids and gases. Truck drivers who drive tankers require extra training because tankers turn over more easily than semis. Tankers filled with gasoline, chemicals, and other kinds of dangerous materials require even more training.

Other trucks move animals, oil, other vehicles, frozen foods, or

Trucks have changed a little over the years! This truck was traveling America's highways back in 1915.

large equipment. Each cargo has its own responsibilities and required training. This makes for a **diverse** set of skills that truck drivers will need on the job. Because of the extra training, these kinds of jobs pay more than a traditional long-haul trucking job.

The History of Trucking

In 1904, only about 700 large trucks were driving around on America's roadways—but by 1914, that number had increased to nearly 25,000. Ten years later, well over 400,000 trucks were being operated each and every day, and in 2000, the Department of Transportation estimated that over 21 million trucks were driving a total over 412 billion miles every year. (That would be equal to driving back and forth to the sun well over 4,000 times!)

CHAPTER 3

How Can I Become a Truck Driver?

"One of the best things about driving a truck (besides the great pay) is how easy and simple it is to become a truck driver," explains Brett Duran, a driver with nearly fifteen years of experience.

The world needs truck drivers, and most experts think there will always be a need for people to do this job. Truck drivers play a necessary role in the economy. When a large amount of anything is bought or sold, someone

A truck driver needs a certain amount of physical strength. Here, a driver is detaching the trailer from the cab.

TRUCK DRIVER

has to move it—and this is where truck drivers come in. Since trucks move most of the goods bought and sold around the world, there will always be a need for people willing to take on the challenging lifestyle of driving trucks.

In most cases, the only education you need is a high school diploma. If you are in good health, then you too can become a truck driver. But don't make the mistake of thinking that it's an easy job!

Is Truck Driving Right for Me?

"If young people are interested in getting a job as a truck driver," explains Brett, "the best thing they can do is learn about the lifestyle, and, as they learn, ask themselves over and over, 'Is truck driving right for me?'"

Truck driving is nothing like any other kind of job. You don't wake up in the same place every day. You don't see the same people every day. A lot of strange and surprising things can happen out on the road.

Brett has "seen it all," but there is one thing that Brett sees far too many times: drivers quitting. "Part of the reason that becoming a truck driver is so simple," Brett says, "is because a lot of drivers quit within their first year. A lot of people who become truck drivers think, 'The pay is good and driving a truck looks easy, so why not?' But they do not take the time to learn or even consider what a difficult job and lifestyle it can be."

According to Brett, the best way to learn about the lifestyle is to talk to people who have made a career out of driving trucks. "The people who quit before the first year might have some bad things to say about

The driver's seat (in the cab) of a truck looks a little different from a car's driver seat! There are more knobs, buttons, and gages to keep track of. The small blue illuminated square near the center of the photo is the automatic climate control. Switches on the dashboard) include marker lamps, headlights, panel dimmer, windshield wipers, the on/off switch for refrigeration, cruise set, cruise on/off, powered mirror, engine brake power, diagnostics, and mirror heat.

it, since they obviously didn't like it. An experienced truck driver will be honest—he or she won't be too positive or too negative about truck driving because, like most things, there are both positive and negative things to say about it. Positive? Adventure, travel, and the open road. Negative? Hardly ever being home, driving in crowded areas, and the difficulty of finding a clean shower."

Of course you will need to love, or at least enjoy, one thing before even considering a trucker's lifestyle. "You *need* to love driving," Brett says. "Driving is what we do, what we live for. It's not always wonderful. Sitting in traffic or driving around a big city can be frustrating, to say the least, but I think every truck driver has felt the peace and calm that can come over you from an open window, a near-empty highway, and some good music to drive by."

Brett grew up in a major city where many young people don't even learn to drive at all. "Where I was from," Brett explains, "getting on a bus or onto the subway was just easier. When I was in high school, none of my friends knew how to drive and none of us had cars. When I go back there today, most of my old friends still don't know how to drive."

Because of this, Brett didn't learn to drive until he went to college. "I went away to college without a clue of what I wanted to do. My college was out in the middle of nowhere, so my second year, I got a driver's license and my parents bought me a car. That was all I needed—a car and some open road—and I knew that driving was for me." Turned out, Brett didn't need his college education after all!

The idea of getting behind the wheel of a car, let alone a fifty-foot semi, might seem scary, but in some states you only have to be fourteen year's old to get a learner's permit, the first step on your way to a driver's license. Brett's advice: "Get your permit. Get your license. Get out there on the road and begin to drive."

Brett makes a good point. Not everyone enjoys driving; some people, for example, think it can be stressful or irritating, and if you don't

like driving, then truck driving certainly isn't for you! On the other hand, if you find yourself sneaking out to a car every time you feel a bit restless, then a life on eighteen wheels might just be the life for you.

What All Truck Drivers Need

While a love of driving and an ability to live the life of a truck driver may make you an ideal **candidate** for the job, every truck driver also needs certain physical abilities in order to be both successful and safe when they are out there driving. The Bureau of Labor Statistics lists five important qualities that every truck driver should have.

- **Hand-eye coordination.** Drivers of heavy trucks and tractor-trailers must be able to coordinate their legs, hands, and eyes together to always be aware of the situation around them and to safely drive such a heavy vehicle.
- **Hearing ability.** Truck drivers need good hearing. Government regulations require that a driver pass a hearing test in order to drive a large truck.
- **Physical health.** Government regulations do not allow people to become truck drivers if they have a medical condition, such as high blood pressure or epilepsy, that may interfere with their ability to operate a truck.

- **Visual ability.** Truck drivers must be able to pass vision tests. Like the hearing test, government regulations require drivers to pass a vision test before they can be hired to drive trucks.

If you have all five of these qualities, then you can consider the lifestyle of a truck driver. But Brett adds two more qualities he thinks all drivers need to make it through even one year on the road:

- **Patience.** Whether it is waiting sometimes hours for your truck to be loaded, driving through a crowded city, being slowed down by heavy traffic, or simply the six hundred miles a day that a truck driver drives on average, a truck driver needs to be patient and calm. People who get frustrated or irritated easily will not only be unhappy with the lifestyle of a truck driver but could potentially put themselves and others on the road in danger with unsafe driving practices.
- **Flexibility.** Life on the road can be one of two things. If you are flexible—able to adapt and change to new situations and events—truck driving means constant adventure. If you are not, truck driving means the stress of never knowing where you will be and what you will be doing the following day. You need to be willing to live each day, sometimes each moment, without knowing what is going to happen next—and this takes flexibility.

According to Brett, beyond these two qualities, truck driving is what you make of it. It can be lonely, especially if you drive alone. You can go days without seeing anyone, let alone someone you know or love—but if you are excited to experience all that the road has to offer, truck driving is a great way to be paid well while doing it.

This student is being trained to fill a tanker that will carry jet fuel.

A Simple Process

Once you're sure you have the qualities listed above and have taken the time to learn all that you can about the lifestyle of a truck driver, then it is a simple process getting started. Most trucking companies will not hire you if you are under the age of twenty-one. Once you're old enough, if you do not have a criminal record—you have not committed any crimes—and have a good work history—you have shown that you can be responsible—then all that you need to get started in the trucking industry is a high school diploma and a driver's license.

Each state has different laws that regulate when you can get a driver's license, but in most states you are able to get a driver's license between the ages of sixteen and eighteen years old. The first driver's license that anyone gets is a Class D license. This kind of license only allows someone to drive small, four-wheeled vehicles. There are other kinds of driver's licenses that allow you to drive other kinds of vehicles, but in order to drive trucks you will need a Commercial Driver's License (CDL).

If you go to a professional driving school, getting your CDL isn't very difficult. At a driving school you will not only learn how to drive a semi but you will also learn all the laws and regulations you'll need to know to drive large trucks. There are two kinds of professional driving schools: private and company-sponsored.

A private driving school costs a few thousand dollars but allows a new driver the freedom of applying to any truck-driving job that he or she wants. This means a higher starting salary and benefits like health insurance and dental insurance.

A company-sponsored driving school is much cheaper than a private driving school, and in some cases, it can even be free. After getting a CDL from one of these company-sponsored schools, though, a new

The Truck Driver Who Reverse-Engineered the Atom Bomb

John Coster-Mullen is a truck driver who truly understands the importance of learning. Coster-Mullen became famous in 2010 and 2011 for becoming the first man, despite attempts by many college-educated people, to "reverse engineer"—a process where someone determines how something worked—one of the two atom bombs dropped on Japan in the Second World War.

What makes Coster-Mullen's discovery so amazing is that despite many countries already having weapons far more powerful than this, the United States government has still not released the plans for exactly how this bomb was built. Therefore, Coster-Mullen, whose research on the atom bomb is considered the most accurate to date, had to determine the exact specifications of the bomb based on old photographs of it both completed and while under production.

According to *The Atomic Trucker: How a Truck Driver "Rebuilt" the Atomic Bomb*, a short documentary made about his life, Coster-Mullen made many of his calculations while sitting in traffic behind the wheel of his truck. Despite his fame and success, Coster-Mullen still drives his semi. He's a great example of someone willing to explore and learn.

Trucks move all sorts of things across the country—even houses!

driver is required to work for the company that trained them for a certain amount of time, usually a year. If a new driver wants to quit in this first year, she will owe the driving school money for training her. This option can be risky, especially if you are not sure that truck driving will be the life for you. If, however, you have done your research and are confident that the consistently changing life of a truck driver is for you, then a company-sponsored driving school makes getting into truck driving so cheap that anyone can afford it.

How Can I Become a Truck Driver?

Tires play a vital role in trucking safety. As part of your training, you will learn to inspect and maintain the truck's tires.

There are many ways to get your CDL—and even if you have to pay for your training, it is cheap compared to a traditional four-year college. This means that getting into the truck driving industry is possible no matter what kind of financial background.

CHAPTER 4

How Much
Can I Make?

"Anyone in the trucking industry will tell you," says Daryl Isaacs, an owner-operator with a little over ten years of experience owning his own truck, "no one drives trucks for the money. But," he adds, "the money is nothing to complain about."

As Brett explained in chapter 3, truck driving is a challenging lifestyle. For some people, no amount of money would be enough to compensate for the lonely hours on the road. But for the men and

If you're a long-haul driver, you'll probably get paid for each mile you drive. The longer you drive, the more money you'll earn.

women who are adventurous and enjoy the lifestyle of trucking, the pay is just an extra bonus for the fulfilling life they have.

High-Level Earnings

"Truck drivers," says Daryl, "are paid a certain amount of money for every mile they drive, plus bonuses—for a quick delivery, for example. I have been working as a long-haul driver for thirty years now, about the last ten of which I have owned my own truck. Leasing was the way to go for me because there was so much less to worry about." As we explained in chapter 2, an owner-operator who leases owns his own truck but works for a larger shipping company.

Daryl continues: "The company I'm driving for pays for all or most of my expenses for gas, oil, licensing, insurance, and about everything else associated with driving a truck hundreds of thousands of miles a year. The only way I could be making more is if I was leasing to a few different companies or had opened my own business—but I tried that for a few years and was not cut out for all of the responsibility. As an owner of a fleet, you could decide not to drive anymore, which makes all of the responsibility easier, but I couldn't give this up. It's my life. I am a truck driver, not a business owner."

As an owner-operator, Daryl is paid sixty-six cents for every mile he drives. All in all, he drives about 100,000 miles a year, which means that Daryl makes about $66,000 per year. When you consider that, according to the Bureau of Labor Statistics, in 2010 the median wage in America was around $33,000 a year, the paycheck Daryl receives seems like a pretty big bonus for a life he loves!

This truck was on the road in the 1950s.

The History of Trucking

The explosion of trucks on the highway happened for a number of reasons. One thing that helped make it happen were new technologies that helped trucks carry more goods and drive much farther. The air-filled tire, for example, which replaced solid rubber tires, not only allowed trucks to carry more weight than before but also made driving far more comfortable for the drivers. Other advances in the technologies of trucks and automobiles included the internal combustion engine, which allowed trucks to travel farther, and air brakes, which allowed for a truck driver to safely and reliably stop a heavy vehicle like a fully loaded semi.

The "sleeper cab" was the next great innovation in truck driving technologies. A sleeper cab, or "sleeper" for short, is a small cabin extended off the back of a semi truck that includes a bed and other minimal needs. Major truck producers such as Peterbilt® began to install sleepers over 40 years ago because of the possibility of saving trucking companies money and allowing drivers to drive for longer distances. The sleeper cab, which can even be big enough to accommodate husband-and-wife driving teams (like Mike and Rhonda from chapter 2), quickly became a necessity for nearly every truck in the long haul shipping industry.

Truckers who drive fuel tankers like this one often make more money because it takes special training to drive hazardous materials safely.

Average Salaries

Any driver who is willing to become experienced, work hard, and take the risk of owning her own truck can hope to make as much as Daryl does. Daryl does make an exceptionally high salary for a truck driver who has not opened his own business, however. The average truck driver makes almost $38,000 a year. But, says Daryl, "When you consider all of the guys who have been out there less than a year and are probably going to quit, and all of the guys who are only doing regional and local driving"—which pays considerably less—"this number is probably a lot higher." By Daryl's second year as a long-haul driver, after only two pay raises, he was already making about $41,000 a year.

The average salary for all truck drivers is a few thousand dollars higher than the national average for all jobs, including those that require a college degree to attain. Clearly, truck driving is a fantastic and well-paying option for those who will be happy and fulfilled by a life on the road!

CHAPTER 5

Looking to
the Future

N o truck driver, at least in the near future, will have to worry too much about losing his job. "Truck drivers have good **job security** for two reasons," says Jill Stein, a former long-haul truck driver who now owns her own fleet of trucks. The first reason, according to Jill, is that since so much of America's economy moves by truck, it is very unlikely that this is going to change any time soon. "The second reason," Jill says, "is that because the truck-driving lifestyle is not for

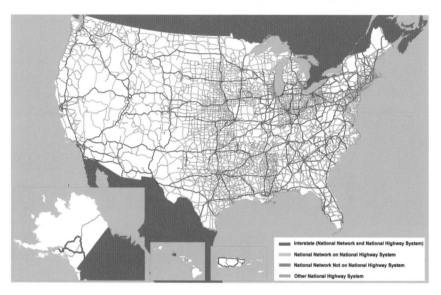

This map shows the vast network of roads where truckers drive across the United States.

Looking at the Words

Knowing you have a secure position at a company and that you will not be laid off for reasons other than making a bad mistake is called **job security**. Job security removes some of the stress of having to worry about keeping a job. It allows a worker to focus more easily on what he or she should be focusing on: working.

everyone, many shipping companies have a very hard time keeping new employees once they have been trained and hired. We have this problem ourselves—we hire someone fresh out of driving school, they seem young and eager, and then a few months in, they tell us that they would like to quit. As an owner of a trucking company, it can be very frustrating, but for truck drivers who enjoy the lifestyle, all of the quitting means that they

will never be out of work and also have the option of looking for better truck driving positions than the one that they have."

On top of that, the Bureau of Labor Statistics predicts that over 300,000 truck-driving jobs will be added to the shipping industry between 2010 and 2020. Job security looks pretty great for this career!

Advancement and Skills

"Advancing as a truck driver" Jill says, "can be difficult and is usually seen in pay raises, better working hours, or better working conditions. At most companies, including ours, after one of our drivers has

Not all truck drivers travel across the country. The driver of this truck works with road-repair crews.

UPS hires drivers for their delivery trucks. The average salary for a UPS driver is $58,653. Drivers need to be able to pass a physical exam that proves they can lift packages—but they don't need a college degree.

driven 60,000 miles for us, we give them a week's paid vacation, and after 120,000 miles, we give them two weeks paid vacation. They can save those hours up or we can pay them for not using them. Also, after 120,000 miles, our drivers are given more choice over when and where they would like to work. After they have shown us that they can be responsible—driving safely and legally—then we give them more freedom and better pay. It is worth it for us to pay safe drivers more than pay all of the fees that an unsafe driver makes us pay."

Another option open to truck drivers looking to advance is to drive for a different company. As Jill mentioned, there are often new openings for truck drivers. If you have experience and a safe driving record, working for a new company can bring a driver better benefits—like medical insurance and dental work—not to mention better pay.

"Another way to advance," Jill says, "is to become an owner-operator." This takes special skills, though. "Owner-operators should have good business sense," Jill says, "as well as a lot of truck driving experience. The more experience you have, the more of the driving business you learn. A successful owner-operator understands how much it really costs to drive a truck or fleet of trucks around the country. Things go wrong—trucks break, accidents happen, tickets are given by police for unsafe driving. There are a lot of costs—gas, insurance, repairs." Knowledge of truck mechanics can allow owner-operators to perform their own routine maintenance and minor repairs.

Part of Jill's success, first as an owner-operator and then as an owner, comes from the classes she took in accounting, business, and business mathematics. "Owner-operators need to understand the industry. The costs can be staggering, and because of this, many owner-operators go out of business—but if you learn a lot about the industry, about business in general, and don't need to run down to the local mechanic anytime anything goes wrong with a truck, then you'll be well on your way to making a great living."

Trucks have come a long way since the days when this 1930 Ford Model AA truck was on the road!

Conclusion

For many people, college is the perfect choice. Not only can it open the doors of certain careers but it is also often the first experience many young people have at living away from home, without the safety and security of their parents. It's an important learning experience.

Unfortunately, many students go to college with no idea about what they would like to do with their lives. They hope this question will be answered for them within the broad opportunities that college offers. Or they feel pressured by their peers or their parents to go to college. Many students leave college still with no idea of what they want from a career. Because of the staggering debt many students have to acquire just to go to college, they may actually be in a worse financial position than before.

The History of Trucking

As trucks were improving, so were America's roads. In 1916, the Federal Aid Road Act was passed, which funded the first major highway systems. Five years later, this bill was extended. The Federal Highway Act began a project to build a 3.2 million-mile national road system. These bills were the beginnings of the roads we know today. They made coast-to-coast travel for a truck possible for the first time.

The people interviewed in this book are men and women who took another route. They are intelligent, driven, and passionate about what they are doing. They all had the willingness to adventure and learn, even if learning didn't mean sitting in a classroom. Ask any one of them and they will tell you that it is some combination of these traits that makes someone successful more than any college degree.

Going to college may be the right choice for you. Or another route may be your best road to success. Either way, explore, learn, and consider every option. Be willing to learn and work hard, no matter where life takes you!

Find Out More

IN BOOKS

Clinton, Susan. *Tractor-Trailer-Truck Driver*. Mankato, Minn.: Capstone Press, 2008.

Thomas, William Davis. *Truck Driver (Cool Careers)*. Milwaukee, Wisc.: Gareth Stevens Publishing, 2009.

Young, Jeff C. *Trucks: The Ins and Outs of Monster Trucks, Semis, Pickups, and Other Trucks*. Mankato, Minn.: Capstone Press, 2010.

ON THE INTERNET

"A History of the Truck and Trucking Industry"
www.randomhistory.com/2008/07/14_truck.html

The Importance of Truck Drivers, "Why America Needs You"
www.gettrucking.com

Trucking Truth, "A Positive Yet Honest View of the Trucking Industry"
www.truckingtruth.com

Bibliography

Aquila, Brett. "Becoming a Truck Driver." TruckingTruth.com. http://www.truckingtruth.com/becoming_truck_driver_nav_page.html (accessed February 6, 2013).

eHow.com. "How Does a Truck Driver Spend a Workday?" http://www.ehow.com/how-does_4569101_truck-driver-spend-work-day.html (accessed February 6, 2013).

JobMonkey.com. "Trucking Careers are Looking Bright." http://www.jobmonkey.com/truckdriving/trucking-careers.html (accessed February 6, 2013).

U.S. Bureau of Labor Statistics. "Heavy and Tractor-Trailer Truck Drivers" http://www.bls.gov/ooh/transportation-and-material-moving/heavy-and-tractor-trailer-truck-drivers.htm (accessed February 6, 2013).

WiseGeek.com. "What Does a Truck Driver Do?" http://www.wisegeek.org/what-does-a-truck-driver-do.htm (accessed February 6, 2013).

Index

About the Author

Connor Syrewicz is a writer and editor from Binghamton, New York. He was raised on Long Island, has a degree in English, and spends most of his time writing and facilitating other creative projects. His interests include art and philosophy, which he actively incorporates into his writing.

Picture Credits